D0431155

Ancient Echoes

Books by Mary Summer Rain

Nonfiction:

Spirit Song
Phoenix Rising
Dreamwalker
Phantoms Afoot
Earthway
Daybreak
Soul Sounds
Whispered Wisdom
Ancient Echoes

Children's:

Mountains, Meadows and Moonbeams

Ancient Echoes
The Anasazi
Book of Chants

Mary
Summer Rain

HAMPTON ROADS
PUBLISHING COMPANY, INC.

Copyright © 1993 by Mary Summer Rain
Cover Art "Anasazi" Copyright © 1990 by Ann Marie

All rights reserved, including the right to reproduce
this work in any form whatsoever, without permission
in writing from the publisher, except for brief passages
in connection with a review.

For information write:

Hampton Roads Publishing Company, Inc.
891 Norfolk Square
Norfolk, VA 23502

Or call: (804) 459-2453
(FAX: (804) 455-8907

If you are unable to order this book from your local
bookseller, you may order directly from the publisher.
Quantity discounts for organizations are available.
Call 1-800-766-8009, toll-free.

10 9 8 7 6 5 4 3 2 1

ISBN 1-878901-87-7

Printed on acid-free paper in the United States of America

For the Ancient Ones,
whose Starborn Heritage still
pulses through the Ancestral Soul
of the living Spirit Clan.

CONTENTS

CONTENTS

CONTENTS

Introduction

This Book of Chants has been manifested because of a deep inner prompting I had to bring forth the beauty and sensitivity of the Anasazi heart. The prayers, chants and songs written on the following pages were unique to the specific Anasazi community known as the Spirit Clan.

Although the acquisition of this knowledge could have come from my personal Advisor and only have taken a couple of days to record, it was strongly suggested that perhaps it would be more meaningful for me if I personally procured the information by extracting it myself through spiritual memory recall. In this way, I would be walking the Sacred Trail that passed through the Sacred Ground where the chants reposed in the Ancient Time where only spirits could perceive their reverberating echoes. Therefore, each entry necessitated an extended period of deep states whereby both the words and the spirit of the words were received. Due to the sacred manner in which this information was ultimately gained, it took well over a year to compile the completed volume.

Because of the language difference and the lack of corresponding English equivalents, it's important for the reader to refrain from trying to read the chants in a metered poem-like rhythm. Since few present-day prayers are actual poems, the reader needs to read these ancient chants as prayers whispered from the heart. Each chant is accompanied by an explanatory background sketch.

Ancient Echoes

Dawn, its sunrise glow of orange reflected on clouds, represented warmth and light. But more than those two physical aspects, the rising sun was an enduring symbol of stability and signified the constant and unchanging facets of nature that were so keenly perceived by the Anasazi People.

Every clan member, elders down to the small children, recognized the spiritual value of what the sunrise meant, and all silently whispered the Dawn Greeting Song as the sun's first colorful rays speared over the eastern horizon.

Dawn Greeting Song

Warm Maker.
Welcome Warm Maker.
I welcome your spirit and invite you to
shine down upon all lands below.
Bless my people with your light.
Bless my people with your warmth.
Warm Maker.
You who are the burning center
of this place, hear my Dawn Greeting Song.
I welcome you. My people welcome you.
Warm Maker. You are the heart and the fire
of my people's new home.
Welcome.

When a woman was in labor, from the first signs of the initial stages, her relatives, accompanied by the Women's Medicine Woman, surrounded the laboring woman and individually recited the Birthing Prayer. This was done while the Women's Medicine Woman went about her work and the female family members each took turns burning cedar and sage within the dwelling. This was done to keep away negative spirits and to keep the room purified for the entry of the new life.

Birthing Prayer

Grandmother, look down and see this woman
of your people. See her pain. See her love for the
child within. Grandmother. Grandmother.
Ease the journey and smooth
this child's path into its new home. Speed this
child's travels toward its new life trail.
Grandmother. Grandmother. On behalf of this
new mother I speak her words with my tongue.
Help this mother and child come together.
Help her bring this new life into
the circle of our people.

Mealtime was a semi-sacred time. This was true for every member of the clan. It didn't matter if the meal was to be taken by a large family gathering or by one living alone. The same procedures were followed by all, for it was Anasazi tradition to respect and honor the animal and plant life that had supplied their sustenance for that meal.

As an additional means of displaying their respect for their continued nourishment, they ate very slowly and were careful not to waste any portions of the food. There were never left-overs, for they cooked only what they were certain would be consumed. In addition, mood at mealtimes were always light, for to eat with anger in one's heart or retain other negative emotions was to dishonor the spirits who had given gifts of their lives. Likewise, no problems were discussed, nor were unhappy situations allowed to enter mealtime conversations.

Meal Thanksgiving Prayer

I honor the life you have given so that I
may be fed. I am thankful for the great
gift you have given me this day.
My heart is full for the sacrifice you have made.
I respect your offering and so will waste
no part of your gift.
My spirit bows to your spirit.

This, naturally, is not the Medicine Man's sacred Healing Way Chant. This one represents the prayer utilized by family members and friends of the ill individual. As with the ceremony done for birthing, cedar and sage were also burned in the sick room by family and friends as they whispered the Healing Way Chant. This was done simultaneously with the Medicine Man's own specific ceremonies.

When the word *Grandfather* was used in Anasazi prayers, songs and chants, the people were referring to a holy entity comparable to the spiritual status of Jesus. Grandfather frequently served as intermediary between the people and the Creator (God) who was differentiated by the terms *The One* or *One Above*.

Healing Way Chant

Hear me, Grandfather.
Hear my words.
Here lies one of your people who is sick and
in great need of your power.
Oh Grandfather, look down. Breathe on this
one of yours. Breathe on this one.
Bless this one with The One's breath
so he will be strong again.
Let him walk in the warming sun.
Let him hear his own laughter.
Let him love and sing again.
Oh Grandfather, heal your people.
Heal this one with the light of The One.

The hunters of the clan were the meat providers. Most often they were men. However, if a woman was seen to possess unusual ability in the hunting skills, she was not looked upon with disfavor, but was welcomed into the Hunter Society.
The hunter went out to replenish the meat supply. They never hunted or killed indiscriminately, but rather used their psyches to determine a specific location to be and simply called to the animals' spirits.

It was important to take only those animals that "appeared" before them after their prayer was repeated over and over. This then signified animals who were fully prepared to give freely of their precious gift of life so that others may live. A hunter dishonored both him/herself and the clan by taking a life that wasn't volunteered.

Hunting Prayer
(a call for animal Give-Aways of self)

Little Ones. Little Ones.
I speak only to the Little Ones who are ready.
I call only the Little Ones who wish to give.
My people are hungry and need to be nourished.
I honor your small life but our little children
cry with empty bellies.
Mothers need food to make their milk.
The old elders are silent in their need to be fed.
Little Ones, hear my call. My spirit calls to
your spirit. If you are ready to give to my
people, come and I will honor you in a sacred
manner that gives you no pain. I will be swift.
Little Ones,
Your gift will give life to my people.
Your gift will sustain us and give us life.

Guilt was not a psychologically manipulative tool among the Anasazi People, but their own advanced intelligence and ancient traditions were so deeply ingrained that whenever someone had negative thoughts or spoke unkindly, they themselves were remorseful — even if nobody else knew about it.

So with all experiences, the transgressor would examine the act, analyze the cause and heartily try to learn a lesson from it. And the individual cleared his/her conscience by privately confessing the deed to the Messenger who in turn, it was believed, took it before The One.

Forgiveness Prayer

Grandfather. Grandfather.
Take my words before The One.
Offer my sign of peace.
Walking this land is new and I have
much to learn here.
My heart has a bleeding wound for
what I did.
I will try to learn from it.
Grandfather. Grandfather.
Take my words before The One.
Offer my sign of love.

All woven material, baskets included, were produced by the Weaver Women of the clan. They were trained in the skill at a young age if they showed promise. These young ones apprenticed with the skilled artisans who did all the clan's weaving. This, we see, was a society of people who neither bartered, traded nor participated in commerce, but rather was one that had separate societies of skilled artisans who produced all the goods for the entire clan.

All artisan societies took great care in their specific creations; therefore, associated songs and prayers were uttered for the purpose of insuring quality though the petitioned guidance of their skilled hands.

Weaver Woman Song

Grandmother. Oh, Grandmother.
Ancient Weaver Woman.
Guide my fingers. Guide my hands.
Bless this work I do this day.
Make it strong. Make it tight.
Give it lasting strength.
Grandmother. Oh, Grandmother.
Ancient Weaver Woman.
Bless this work I do this day.

Clan elders gathered once a week at the time of twilight to discuss community affairs and assess its progress. These wizened council members consisted of the most talented individuals of each society within the clan. Men and women. There were representatives of the Weaver Woman Society, Hunter Society, Builder Society, etc. In this democratic manner, the elders who were solely responsible for the clan's direction could receive valuable input from all aspects of the community. It was, in essence, a small-scale United Nations-style council.

Council Fire Prayer

Together we come to make decisions.
Together we come to consult one another.
Together we come to speak of the people.
Together we come to lead in a sacred manner.
One Above. One Above.
Give us wisdom this night.
Make our words true.
Make our words fair.
One Above. One Above.
Guide your people this night.

Throughout time, in almost all American Indian cultures, each tribe had an individual who was designated as the historian so the people's past would always be verbally recorded in tales and stories to be repeated verbatim and handed down from generation to generation.

The Anasazi were no different in this manner, for they too had their appointed Storyteller, only this elder recounted an ancestral tradition of heritage that was founded in the stars.

Legend Teller's Prayer

Grandfather. Ancient Grandfather.
Keeper of the Heritage.
Guard my tongue. Hear my voice.
Guide the stories of my heart.
Grandfather. Ancient Grandfather.
Keep the sounds of truth near me.
Let my ears be open.
Hear my prayer to ask that my people
never forget who they are or where they
came from.
Grandfather. Ancient Grandfather.
Keeper of the Heritage.
Guard my tongue. Keep it true.

The members of the Spirit Warrior Society were uniquely different from all the other established society members. They were responsible for the spiritual protection of the clan. These highly respected warriors were not trained to do physical battle, but rather the far more dangerous type that took place on the Unseen Plain of the spirit.

The people were highly enlightened in spiritual matters and considered the dark forces as their greatest and deadliest foe.

Spirit Warrior Chant
(for strength and courage against dark forces)

Oh Great One Above.
Bring strength to me and keep
my power strong.
Dark ones keep from us.
Shield us from their face.
I am not afraid to fight.
Oh Great One Above.
I am Spirit Warrior of the People.
I guard my people from the dark ones.
I will protect with my life.
Oh Great One Above.
I am Spirit Warrior.
I will shield with The One's Light.
I am not afraid to fight.

Each individual clan member was taught from the earliest age about spiritual concepts. Elementary lessons included the necessity of utilizing one's own personal light of protection. This was considered a means of great power and all members were aware they had the spiritual capability of protecting themselves by energizing visions of their own shields being infused with great power.

Several times a day and whenever someone felt the need, the Power Shield Prayer was silently said while the individuals envisioned themselves encapsulated in a sphere of blinding light.

Power Shield Prayer
(for personal protection)

I am strength and the strength is strong.
Strong is my power.
My power protects me.
I see the power around me.
From inside it comes to encircle me in
its light.
The light I see is shining like the sun.
I am strength and the strength is strong.
Strong is my power.
My power protects me.

When any food was cooked, the preparer (male or female) quietly said words over the fire. This is not indicative of a belief in a fire spirit per se, but rather in thoughtful thanksgiving for the fire's raw convenience. And a morsel of the food was tossed into the flames as a simple token of the cook's appreciation.

Here we clearly see that the Anasazi took nothing for granted in their daily lives. They were aware in life and fully appreciated everything that made life easier for them — even the flame of the fire that cooked their meals.

Cooking Fire Song

Fiery Spirit.
Keeper of the Flame.
Burn bright and long.
Heat this food and cook it well.
Bless it with your breath.
Fiery Spirit.
Keeper of the Flame.
I gift you with this offering.
In a sacred way I honor you.

The Clan Prayer was reverently said by all the members in the late evening. Historically speaking, they were aware of their beginnings and why they were on earth for a designated span of time. They were ever mindful of their purpose and, therefore, were also ever mindful to pray for guidance and protection upon the new and strange land.

They were not unaware of how easy it would be to forget their purpose, so then, it was important to keep this before their minds on a daily basis.

Clan Prayer

We raise our eyes to home and ask that
our Grandfather Above not forget his people.

We raise our spirits with hope and ask that
The One protects us from afar.

We pray for direction upon this strange land.
We pray the vision will be fulfilled and our
foot traces keep hidden from our enemies.

Grandfather Above, protect your people.
Grandfather Above, guide your people.

Since the Anasazi were such a unique group of people, they knew their young children would be the ones to be the future and carry on *if* the clan was permitted to remain beyond the designated amount of time.

This then was a very strong underlying purpose for them — that of teaching, nurturing, and protecting their children.

Child Chant
(for protection of clan's children)

I know how you love the children.
They are our future.
They are the innocent ones.
They are the hope of our people.
One Above.
Great One Above.
Help us watch over the children.
One Above.
Great One Above.
Help us watch over the children.

Each clan individual, whether young or old, was raised to walk through life upon the Wisdom Trail. This doesn't mean they had to always strive for high intelligence, for they already knew there was a deep chasm between intelligence and wisdom. They strove for inner counsel that spawned truth, fairness and right choices. This then is the wisdom prayed for.

Wisdom Way Prayer
(for personal inner wisdom)

May wisdom come into my heart.
May wisdom enter my soul.
May I speak the wisdom words.
And walk the Wisdom Way.
Guide my thoughts.
Guide my tongue.
May truth live here in my heart.
May Wisdom show the Way.

Marriage ceremonies were simple affairs. Everyone gathered around the Central Grounds while the appointed Chief Clan Elder, together with the couple's parents, bonded the two together in a simple prayer said aloud in unison. Afterward, the entire community gave gifts and celebrated the happy event. Later, the newlyweds were escorted to a freshly-prepared dwelling that was completely furnished and outfitted by the community members.

Marriage Song

Grandfather. Grandfather.
Look down on these two.
Gift them with forever love.
Bless their trail with peace.
Give them fruitful unions.
And many healthy children.
Grandfather. Grandfather.
Look down on these two.
Bond them to each other.
And gift them with strong love.

Throughout the year, nature generously supplied a wide variety of growing things that could be utilized in a multitude of ways. Some of these grew in waterways, some on the plains and deserts. Gathering parties journeyed away from the community to collect whatever was in season. Entire families joined in and traveled to assist the main groups.

When the gathering actually commenced, prayers were said as each individual joined in the work to unearth the specimens. These prayers, like the mealtime prayers, gave honor and respect to the lifeforce that had been given as a gift of nourishment to the people. The gentle uprooting of cattail, the gathering of grass, the collection of piñon nuts, all done only *after* the prayer was said.

Here we see that the high respect for all living things so dominated the Anasazi culture that it was tightly woven in their overall spiritual and historical tradition.

Gathering Time Prayer

Small spirits of desert and plain,
Small spirits of rivers and stream,
We come to harvest your goodness.
We come to gather your gifts.
In honor and respect,
In a sacred way,
We come to harvest your gifts.

The community dwellings were like a complete city that combined and encompassed all the structures required of a productive and synergic society of people. As such, the construction of these buildings was considered to be of paramount concern for both the safety and protection of the people.

The builders, therefore, shouldered the heavy burden and responsibility of insuring the longevity of their architectural skills. And being fine craftsmen, they had an associated chant that sporadically accompanied their work process.

Building Chant

Hands shape the stone.
Mind gives it strength.
Soul gives it power.
The One gives it life.

Stone for longevity.
Strength for protection.
Power for safety.
Life for purpose.

Anasazi People believed in the sanctity of the family unit. They encouraged a unique openness to be shared between family members whereby separatism of both gender and status were virtually nonexistent concepts. Husband and wife shared equally in household activities and both were responsible for their children's education.

The children were urged to expand their intellectual horizons and innate curiosity by asking questions on any subject they wished. All members participated in frequent family outings and most clan ceremonies.

Family Prayer

May the love between us be strong.
May the trust between us be whole.
And may the words between us be true.

May our eyes see one another.
May our ears hear one another.
May our hearts touch one another.
And may our souls hold one another.

Everyone in the clan community was familiar with spiritual manifestations of personal visions. These were perceived as typically normal occurrences and those experiencing them were not considered special or unusual or raised to a designated status of being holy or sacred. This is because visions were common to the people; however, visions themselves were looked upon as sacred messages and directives generated through Grandfather from the One Above.

Whenever someone had a vision, whether it be from elder or child, male or female, the individual visited the Chief Clan Elder to share what had been communicated. In turn, the wise elder interpreted the message and shared it during the Council Fire Gatherings.

Vision Way Chant
(for pure visions)

Grandfather. Grandfather.
Keep false visions from my sight.
Keep my eyes open, bright.
Whether it be night or day,
Show me what you wish to say.

Grandfather. Grandfather.
If you wish it to be me,
Say the words, I will see,
What we need to know,
of visions that you show.

A strongly-held tenet of the Anasazi spiritual belief system was the concept that dream images were cognitive and precognitive messages from the dreamer's higher self. This then was considered a sacred and highly personal tool that shed valuable insights onto present-day life situations and also served as a window that often gave a view of the future.

When a clan member felt a dream was particularly meaningful for the community at large, the individual would confide in the Chief Clan Elder who would interpret the symbology and make his determination.

Dreaming Way Chant
(for dream inspiration and understanding)

Vision with night wings,
Show me the way.
My night eyes are open.

Visions with night wings,
Bring me the signs,
And help me to know.

Visions with night wings,
Help me to see,
the truth within me.

For a people who were hunters and gatherers, it was important to have an abundant variety of sources throughout all seasons to harvest from. Therefore it was a wise and prudent people who recognized the wisdom of praying for the myriad crops. These were not crops of their own hands, but were nature's own wild ones of field and valley.

Throughout the year, the community members sang the Planting Song which was a prayer for the Earth Mother's crops to be fruitful and reseed.

Planting Song
(for nature to reseed itself)

Oh gentle Wind Spirit.
Blow your gentle breath over the land.
Sing your song through valleys and plains.
Scatter the seeds. Scatter the seeds.

Oh kind Wind Spirit.
Scatter seeds upon the land.
Take them far. Take them far.
Bring them near. Bring them near.

Little seeds. Little seeds.
Burrow deep and safe.
Drink the rain. Drink the rain.
And grow to reach the sun.

The Sun Chant was a thanksgiving prayer that recognized the gifts of the sun. As stated earlier, the Anasazi appreciated all the simple things in life others tend to take for granted or ignore altogether. The clan community was grateful for the sun's light and warmth and, if they were grateful for something, they expressed that emotion in prayer, song or chant.

This was a general chant that had no specific time of day associated with its recitation. Whenever clan members felt particularly appreciative for the sun's gifts, they freely verbalized their inner feelings.

Sun Chant

Blessed Sun, Oh Blessed Sun.
I thank you for your warm heart.
Blessed Sun, Oh Blessed Sun.
I thank you for your spirit light.

Warm my face.
Warm our land.
Shine your smile down.
Blessed Sun, Oh Blessed Sun.
I thank you for your smile.

Most of the Anasazi communities were constructed upon dry and arid terrain in the Southwest — not all, but most. This then frequently necessitated a call for the heavens to unleash its life-restoring waters. The call for falling waters was not only directed to the people's needs, for the whole of the clan community held deep concern for all of nature that thirsted upon the parched and cracked land. The Anasazi prayed for rainwaters to fall for themselves and also for all of nature straining to preserve itself.

Rain Prayer

Grandfather. Grandfather.
See how your people thirst with dry tongues.
Look upon our lands that crack and split.
Hear the growing things that strain to stay green.

Grandfather. Grandfather.
Ask The One to use the power,
To blow and move the clouds.
Tell him how the people thirst,
And how the land needs water.

Grandfather. Grandfather.
We call the rain. We call the rain.
We call the heaven's water.

Not only did the Anasazi think to pray for nature's crops to reseed, and the rain to water the seeds, but they also knew it was important to also include a prayer for nature's plants to be fruitful. Many plants would appear to grow well, but then during the harvest and gathering times, the fruits would be scanty or never ripen the way they should. So it was important to offer some type of prayer for the wild botanical crops the Earth Mother provided in her many gardens.

Blossom Time Song
(for healthy fruits to harvest)

Grandmother. Oh, Grandmother.
Keeper of the earth.
Keeper of the garden.
Nourish all the growing life,
Of valley, plain and desert.

Grandmother. Oh, Grandmother.
Keeper of the earth.
Keeper of the garden.
Bring health to all the growing life,
And bless us with their fruits.

Because of the advanced intelligence of the Anasazi ancestors, their spiritual belief system was one that aligned with the Precepts of the Law of One. In other words, they were spiritually enlightened people. This then accounted for the Old Spirit Prayer, for although the title may appear to be a prayer for the elderly, it is misleading because the prayer is for the clan's newborns who enter with old spirits. Therefore, the people prayed for the old spirit to retain its knowledge. The prayer also warmly welcomed the spirit into their midst.

Old Spirit Prayer
(for a newborn)

Old Spirit. Old One.
We welcome you this day.
We open our hearts, open our arms,
To your being that has come.

Old Spirit. Old One.
We welcome you to home.
We pray your light will join with ours,
And we gift you with our love.

Welcome Old Spirit.
Welcome Old One.
Welcome to your new home.

A married Anasazi woman was not relegated to a lower status than her husband. Nor was she looked upon as the workhorse of the marriage as was the case in many later tribe societies. The couple shared duties; however, the woman took great feminine satisfaction in performing the more womanly aspects of the household such as the cooking, sewing, and decorating the dwelling to give it a well-organized and homey feeling. Caring well for her husband and his home was a natural instinct borne of love.

Wife's Prayer

Grandmother. Oh, Grandmother.
Make me stay a good wife.
Guide my days, guide my nights.
Make me stay a good wife.

Make my meals be nourishing.
And our home be full of love.
Guide my hands when I sew.
And keep us one at night.
Grandmother. Oh, Grandmother.
Make me keep him happy.
Guide my days, guide my nights.
Make me stay a good wife.

Although the married Anasazi man was not perceived as being "unmanly" when he shared the household chores with his wife, he was most often happiest when actively participating in the role of provider and protector. As has been seen, women too had hunting skills, but they were more the exception than the rule and the hunters were the ones the clan community depended upon for their daily sustenance and stores of food supplies.

Whether the husband be hunter, spirit warrior, builder, council elder, artisan or watcher (warrior), he still took great satisfaction in coming home to his wife. And he too uttered a prayer to insure the life he shared with his wife would remain as unchanged as possible.

Husband's Prayer

One Above. One Above.
Keep me strong. Keep me whole.
Guide my days, guide my nights.
Keep our blankets warm with love.

One Above. One Above.
Let me protect, let me guard,
My wife and home from harm.
Let me provide, let me supply,
All our needs of home.

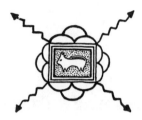

Because the children of the Anasazi community were perceived as its most precious treasure, all women were considered foster mothers to them all. The women, young and old, single and married, loved the children of others as their own. Although the little ones were securely bonded to their birth mothers, spending time with the other women gifted them with warm feelings of being an integral part of the community family and loved by all.

Biological mothers were comforted by the fact that they could be away from the community to hunt or harvest without fear or concern for their children's care. There were always other women to temporarily open their home to any child.

By this we see that the Anasazi People were extremely nurturing and protective of their children.

Mother's Chant

May my little ones always be my heart's treasure.
May I bring smiles and laughter to their faces.
I pray I will always hear their words — their
Spoken and unspoken words.

May my little ones always feel safe and loved.
May I teach them true and guide them straight.
I pray I will always provide their needs — their
Seen and unseen needs.

We will hold hands and go walking.
We will talk and sing the songs.
We will sit in the moonlight silence,
To watch our star and dream of home.

The elderly members of the clan community were honored in a way no other segment of the society was. They were accorded the highest respect and regard, for they were perceived as possessing a great degree of experience and wisdom.

When it came time for each society to disperse their goods, such as food, clothing and other supplies, the elderly members were always surveyed before others. They were deferred to in all things. Their words and thoughts held weight and were intently listened to. The elderly were encouraged to actively participate in all aspects of the community activities and affairs. Because they did, the Anasazi never experienced a Grandmother or Grandfather who died of loneliness or a broken heart.

Grandmother/Grandfather Prayer
(for elder's longevity)

Great Grandfather. Great Grandmother.
Look upon our old ones and keep them well.
Gift them with long lives and many happy smiles.
Show our old ones how much
we love and honor them.
Bring them strength of mind and body.

Great Grandmother. Great Grandfather.
Look upon our old ones and keep them safe.
Gift them with clear eyes and strong minds.
Show our old ones how much we care.
Bring them comfort and peace of heart.

A couple's discovery that they had eyes for one another was never a private thing between them. Their secret of a new love blossoming was written on their faces and sparked from their eyes for all to see. And the clan members would grin with knowing looks as the couple tried to temper their affection in public. This was to avoid the old women who twittered behind their hands, and the teasing done by young men and women. It was all to no avail though. Once the couple's feelings were discovered, no amount of feigned nonchalance sheltered them from the community's shared enthusiasm. Like the rains in late summer, like the sun on winter days, a budding romance was a reason for joy — for everyone.

New Love Chant
(for love to endure)

Heart beats like dancing drums.
Blood rushes like river waters.
Mind flutters here and over there,
Back to the face of my love.

I call power to this love.
I call life to this love.
Burn bright heart flame.
Burn strong and warm and long.

Personal responsibility was greatly encouraged, for each clan member was solely answerable for their daily decisions and the individual thought processes that led to those decisions. It was thought that people who continually consulted the elders or the shaman indicated personal insecurities about their own mental processes of reasoning thought, logic and deduction. This didn't infer that advice was frowned upon, for everyone occasionally sought advice of the elders, but the *dependency* upon their continual counsel was perceived as an inner weakness of an individual.

Therefore, members sought their own counsel from the Within Path to discover solutions to problems, valuable insights and personal guidance. In this manner did all strive to tap into their own inner knowledge in a sacred manner.

Clear Eyes Chant
(for inner perspective through the Within Path)

May my eyes be opened to see the Path
Before me.
May the Way be clear.
May my feet be quick to walk the Path
Before me.
May the Way be clear.
May my spirit know the Within Path.
May the Way be clear and eyes be open.

All clan members understood the importance of keeping to their ancestral traditions. This was not only because they wanted to keep their nature identity pure, but because they realized the uniqueness of the entire Anasazi group as a people. Historically, they were well aware of their starborn beginnings; consequently, it was a high priority for them to nurture and preserve their unprecedented relationship with other intelligences. In this manner, the connective bond between life on earth and life outside the earth was an ever-renewing aspect of their daily lives.

Straight Path Prayer
(to stay aligned with clan traditions)

Our trails lead to and through nature.
All nature is within our beings.
Let the People never forget this bond
That binds us to all living things.
May our hearts be home to tradition,
And our spirits circle the Hoop
That binds Spirit Clan to all that is.
Such is our Way.
Such we will hold sacred.

Friendships were special relationships that were openly displayed. It was not forbidden for grown males and females to be close friends or to have close associations. Community mores stressed openness between all its members and that encompassed every man, woman and child.

Friends who eventually became very close were perceived as individuals who possessed an additional measure of trust and love for their fellow men. Generally speaking, gaining many close associations was viewed with great acceptance, for the clan itself strove to include each member in this circle of *all* being bonded with each other.

Friends Prayer

My heart is your heart.
My soul holds you dear.

I pray for you.
I care for you.

Friend of mine,
My special friend,
May Grandfather keep you in his heart.

My heart is your heart.
Friend of mine,
My soul holds you dear,
My special friend.

Although the clan itself, as a whole community, had a singular group purpose to strive for, each individual also had separate ideals of purpose which they needed to work toward. This is directly associated with the personal visions which spiritually guided individuals along their own paths for their specific purposes. One's vision created a strong mind-set whereby the man or woman intently focused his or her entire life on.

Since these personal visions were so important in one's life, it naturally followed that all members prayed for their footfalls to remain true and never veer from their purposes. To do so was seen as a sign of weakness and greatly dishonored both an individual and the conceptual Spirit of Visions.

Vision Trail Chant

(to remain true to one's vision path)

Vision Spirit.
Message Maker.
Keep me strong,
Keep me true,
To my vision Trail.

Vision Spirit.
Message Maker.
Keep before me,
Signs that show,
My feet upon my Path.

As differentiated from the Straight Path Prayer, this particular prayer didn't address Starborn traditions as practiced by the earthbound Anasazi, but rather dealt with the *ancient* Starborn Ways that, for one technical reason or another, couldn't be duplicated on earth because of various environmental constraints.

So although the clan lacked hands-on practice of these unique traditions, they strove to keep the reality of them alive within the hearts of the people.

Star Path Prayer
(for remembrance of Starborn Ways)

In our breasts live Ancient Ways that
Pulse with each heartbeat.

In our minds live Starborn Ways that
Shine with firelight.

In our souls live Sacred Ways that
Rest within our power.

Heartbeat of breast,
Firelight of mind,
Power of soul,
Keeps the Starborn Way.

As a native community, the Anasazi had relatively few enemy sources. In their perspective, nature itself could be seen as an enemy if it presented the people of the community as a whole with negative conditions such as bitter winters, scarce meat supply, dry summers and poor harvests.

Generally the people prayed the Enemy Way Prayer to send healing energies of a rosy light of friendship and goodwill that was pointedly directed toward anything or anyone who was perceived as darkly affecting an individual or the community at large in a negative manner.

Enemy Way Prayer
(for one's enemies)

Healing Light,
Light of Power,
Come before my eyes.

Healing Power,
Power of Light,
Grow before me now.

Light of Power,
Light of Love,
Go seek my enemy.

Circle him. Circle him.
Make a Hoop of Light,
Around my enemy,
To turn him back from me.

Healing Light,
Light of Power,
Come before my eyes.

Whenever an individual had to travel or a society
group prepared to journey for the purpose of hunting
or gathering, the community joined with the Chief
Clan Elder in earnestly reciting the Far Journey Chant.
This was repeated five times with accompanying drum-
mers and designated singers who rhythmically main-
tained the proper cadence for the chant.

Far Journey Chant
(for journey safety)

We far journey,
We far travel,
Over new trails,
Upon new paths.

Keep us well,
Guide us true,
Over new trails,
Upon new paths.

Bring us back,
See us home,
Where loved ones wait,
Our safe return.

The Ancestor Star Prayer was said specifically for the clan's starborn relations and friends who were not a part of the earth community. It was a heartfelt prayer that served as a connective bond between the separated peoples.

Likewise, the Anasazi counterparts had a similar prayer they intoned for their absent family on earth.

Ancestor Star Prayer
(for Star Relations)

Grandfather. Oh, Grandfather.
Our relations live in our hearts.
Our far brothers and sisters are missed,
And we feel their place in our souls.

Keep them safe and well, Grandfather.
Guide their long journeys and keep
Them from harm.
Our days and nights are filled
With thoughts of love for them.

Grandfather, Oh, Grandfather.
All our relations live in our hearts.

This chant differed from the Star Path Prayer. This one was for the prime purpose of preserving the sacred spiritual ways which included crystal power, healing methods of sound and color, nature calling techniques, animal communication and personally developed abilities present-day science would still deny...magic, if you will. But in actuality, nothing more than a high understanding of physics.

These enlightened and advanced practices were the foundation of the Spirit Clan's spiritual belief system, for they were what clearly distinguished them from other native sects sharing the earth during that time frame.

Sacred Way Chant
(to hold to sacred spirit ways)

Power of Light, Power of Sound,
Colors, Nature, Stones,
Dwell within the nights and days,
Of our Sacred Ways.

Spirits of Nature, Spirits All,
Crystals and the Totems,
Speak. Teach. Stay
Our Sacred Spirit Way.

Unity and oneness of the community members of the clan was a given. However, another given not as obvious was the stressing of each person's unique individuality that was always, and in many various ways, encouraged to bud forth and blossom.

Unlike many community living groups today, the Anasazi tried to nurture each individual's unique personality in an effort to avoid a homogenized unexpressive society. Therefore, all members were strongly urged to openly express themselves by way of opinions, suggestions, moods and inner perceptions.

Straight Face Chant
(to always be yourself)

I will speak my words.
I will think my thoughts.
Deeds I do will be mine.

I will open my heart.
I will walk my way.
Trails I tread will be mine.

True Words. True Thoughts.
I will show my face.
True Heart. True Way.
I will show my face.

Since the sacredness and uniqueness of this particular song would be a desecration to repeat due to its sacred sensitivity, the *general* Medicine Way Song has been received for public disclosure.

This specific song was sung softly — as a whisper — by the medicine woman herself and was brought forth for ceremonies conducted for minor illnesses and lesser injuries.

Medicine Way Song

Mother of Mothers. Grandmother.
Blow your breath into my mouth.
Let your spirit fill my being,
And bring your power down.

Grandmother. Mother of Mothers.
Circle me in your light.
Guide my hands. Open my eyes.
And circle your power around.

The Brother Calling Chant was recited for the sole purpose of initiating a physical communion with the clan's relatives and friends who were not present on earth. This chant was accompanied by crystal work that was aligned with coordinated sound vibrations.

Brother Calling Chant

I hold the stone.
I call my relations.
Hear me. Hear me.

Hot grows the stone.
Shining lights. Singing. Singing.
Star Ones hear my call.

The stone breathes.
The stone quakes.
Brothers, hear my call.

The fruitful Harvest Song was not sung for the plants, but was sung for those who would be joining the Gathering Society when they all traveled away from the community for the purpose of harvesting the Earth Mother's growing bounties.

The song was not particularly meant as a prayer of protection for the travelers, but rather one that beseeched The One to grant a harvesting success and bring back full baskets.

Fruitful Harvest Song

Earth Mother. Earth Mother.
Maker of all seed.
Give bounty to desert and plain.
Bring gifts of health and life.

Earth Mother. Spirit of Life.
Keep our baskets full.
We thank you for your loving care.
Keep our baskets full.

Earth Mother. Life Maker.
Nourish all of nature.
Keep all of nature strong.
We thank you for your care.

The Anasazi perception of darkness was not so simple as being confined to the narrow reference to nighttime. Darkness to them meant mental blocks to creativity, spiritual veils that temporarily seemed to hamper visions, blocks to problem resolutions, an onset of poor reasoning or logic, or any other type of sudden interruption of one's clear perceptual aspects.

The Owl Way Chant called upon the Owl Spirit to share its sharp night sight and pierce through the darkness the chanter was experiencing. To the Spirit Clan, the owl symbolized high wisdom, keen perception and the dispeller of dark forces.

Owl Way Chant
(for perceptual clarity through darkness)

Owl One.
Spirit of Night.
Come to share your sight,
With one who cannot see.

Owl One.
Spirit of the Night.
Part the veil of night,
For one who cannot see.

Owl One.
Spirit of Night.
Take wing and rise,
To share your spirit eyes.

Owl One.
Spirit of Night.
Fly unto me,
And help me to see.

The clan community, because of its origins, possessed personal (spiritual and physical) knowledge of many intelligent races of beings from outside their earthly realm. Being frequented by these various entities was the prime reason for including a special all-inclusive prayer for them in their repertoire of songs, chants and prayers. This specific prayer was a general one for the health and protection of all Star Nation People.

Night Sky Prayer
(for health and protection of Star Nation)

Lights of Night.
Sky Campfires.
Burn bright to light the way.
Keep our relations.
Watch our relations.
Guide them night and day.

Lights of Night.
Sky Campfires.
Burn strong on paths afar.
Lead our People,
Help our People,
Journey though the stars.

The reality of personal spirit journeys was a foundational spiritual belief of the Spirit Clan community, for the manifestation of these journeys was what solely freed the individual from their physical confinement of the bounds earth brought to them. Spirit journeys were encouraged; however, it was also stressed that these travels be for productive purposes and never for frivolous fancies (except on occasion when an individual was feeling the weight of earthly vibrations).

When young children reached a personal understanding of the concept, they began their journeys with an elder accompanying them. Usually by the age of twelve they were accomplished enough to travel solo.

Spirit Winging Chant
(for prompting spirit journeys)

Spirit Within.
Breathe the Power.
Open your eyes.
See the lights.

Spirit Within.
Breathe the Power.
Open you ears.
Hear the sounds.

Spirit Within.
Breathe the Power.
Spread your wings,
And rise up free.

Complete observation and its natural flow of continuum into Soul Flight was frequently practiced for various purposes. When it was utilized, the individual sang the Eagle Calling Song that attracted an eagle to the singer's area. The singer then intently observed the bird and smoothly shifted his or her consciousness to it, thereby, in essence, sharing the raptor's physical aspects.

Eagle Calling Song

Winged One. Sky Spirit.
Hear my call.
Hear my voice.
Come, Winged One.
Come to share your
Sky with me.

Sky Spirit. Winged One.
See my spirit.
See my heart.
Come to share your
Soul with me.

Manipulation or control of anything was never the Anasazi Way; rather, they viewed their natural abilities as being a giving and sharing. Working with weather elements was a synergic feat whereby nature worked in *cooperation* with the clan. Spirits of Nature frequently cooperated in aiding the people.

The Wind Way Chant was performed when the direction of wind currents required alteration, such as wind shift needed during a grass fire, or the calling up of the winds to scatter wild seeds. This chant was also performed when the Wind Spirit was needed to carry specific messages to an Anasazi Clan Chief in another community some distance away.

Wind Way Chant
(to stir the winds)

Breath Maker,
Hear the voice of the People.
Look into our hearts.
See into our souls.
Come, Wind Spirit, come this way.

Breath Maker,
Breathe over the land.
Bring your Spirit near.
Touch us with your Power.
Come, Wind Spirit, come this way.

Breath Maker,
We call to you.
Come. Come to us.
Hear our voices say
Come, Wind Spirit, come our way.

Clearly, this prayer needs no explanatory sketch, for the clan was an extremely peaceful community and its societal foundation rested solidly upon Peace itself. Therefore, the Peace Prayer was directed toward their outer world in general which included all life on earth as well as that above and around it. This "life" encompassed all spirit entities as well.

Peace Prayer

May harmony dwell in the hearts of all People,
Within and between them let peace be their Way.

May thoughts and deeds be gentle and kind,
And trails be straight, paths be true.

May starlight show the way at night,
And dark clouds never stay the day.

May nature thrive upon this land,
And Peace abide in the Sacred Manner.

This prayer may, initially, appear to be a self-serving one that would also, on the surface, seem hypocritical. But this prayer is not recited so the people could have an abundant hunting supply; its purpose is for harmony and for a plentiful sustenance for the animal species so their young ones will not starve, but grow strong. It asks for order within the animal kingdom and that their spirits dwell within their own power.

Four-Legged Prayer

Four-leggeds large and small,
May Grandmother keep you in her heart,
And wrap her arms about you,
To keep you safe and well.

Four-leggeds of wood and plain,
May Grandmother keep you in her soul,
And gift you with her bounty,
To keep you fed and warm.

My four-legged relations,
Feel my spirit touch,
Know my heart loves,
Hear my prayer for you.

It was believed that all things had a spirit force of energy. These, of the Earth Mother, were known as Nature Spirits. And nature spirits possessed a unique sense of knowledge. Their specific properties contained individualized aspects which could then be communicated to people who heard and understood.

In particular, the spirit force of the Standing Stones (mesas) possessed a unique vibratory rate of such refined frequency that they served as a communication linkage to the clan's Star People. So then, the Standing Stones Chant was a prayer for clarity of messages received from their living essence — their nature's spirit.

Standing Stone Chant

Spirit of the Mesa Stone,
Here I stand — alone.
My ears are open to hear,
All within your sacred sphere.

Spirit of the Mesa Stone,
Tell what must be known.
My heart is open to believe,
The sacred message I receive.

Spirit of the Mesa Stone,
Softly does your voice intone,
Words and wisdom of the Ages,
From the breath of our Star Sages.

Thunder, being a powerful aspect of nature, contains an energy force. The Spirit Clan communicated with this force also, for there truly were Beings behind all the thunder.

Even today, various kinds of star vehicles will emit a sound very much like thunder when they're taking off or landing. Sometimes they sound like a sonic boom. Because these vehicles are frequently shrouded in rain clouds, they can (and do) come and go at will without detection.

Thunder Song

Thunder Maker. Thunder Maker.
Cloud Bringer and Earth Quaker.
Spirits of the wild Storm.
Power of the Sky Starborn.

I stand before your might and force,
To join within your spirit source.
Rolling thunder, clouds define,
A sign our spirits intertwine.

Spirits of the wild Storm.
Power of the Sky Starborn.
I stand before your might and force,
To join within your spirit source.

Whether the belief in true nature spirits is accepted or not among the present-day general public cannot affect the Anasazi belief in the miniature people who populated our earth in forests and deserts alike. These little ones were extremely benevolent and, more often than not, came to assist the clan in whatever way they could. They were most often called for the simple purpose of companionship which displayed a camaraderie of species living upon and sharing the same lands.

Little Spirits Chant

Little Ones of Night and Day.
Little Ones of North and South.
Ones Within and Ones Without.
Hear my call. Hear my voice.

Little Ones of Nature's Way.
All the Unseen Ones.
Little Ones of East and West.
Hear my call. Hear my voice.

This prayer involved a mini-ceremony that was reverently performed in each dwelling every evening. It involved the placing of sacred herbs into the family's altar fire while reciting the prayer.

Each family member old enough to speak joined in the voicing of the words that prayed for a peaceful night for all clan members and life everywhere. Because of the prayer's purpose, it was performed during nature's golden moments of tranquility between daylight and darkness when Grandmother Earth herself seemed to be praying.

Sun-Going-Down Smoke Prayer
(Eventide Prayer)

Our prayers rise in this sacred smoke.
Our hearts are full. Our hearts are full.

We join our voices with Grandmother's,
In her sacred silent time.

Our prayers rise in this sacred smoke,
That carries love for all of life.

May life of earth, upon and within,
Sleep safe in Grandmother's heart.

Twice a year (spring and fall) a festive ceremony was held in the community's Common Ground area. This was to honor the clan's star relations and these were symbolized by the Great Phoenix which the people represented in the form of feathered masks and intricate costumes.

There was much gay celebration, for the entire ceremony was an enactment of the final day when their star relations would return to take them back to their own world. Drumming represented the thunder sounds the star vehicles made. The masks designated their star relations. Feathered wings of costumes symbolized their flight. And the chanting and dancing denoted their great joy at finally returning home.

Phoenix Dance Song
(for Clan's return to Starborn Home)

Thunder Maker. Winged Phoenix.
We await your final visit.
Star Brothers. Star Sisters.
We prepare our last journey.

We wear our best and celebrate,
Our Far Journey from here.
The Leaving Time that is to come,
Gives us joy and hope.

Star Relations from the sky,
We celebrate this day,
To celebrate the final day,
When you come to take us home.

Natural forces of the earth were not a mystery to the Anasazi, for they were not a primitive people in the true sense of the word. They were a highly intelligent society who had the advanced knowledge of their star relations, but were placed upon a primitive land where their technology was virtually useless as far as practicality. Yet they were not left completely powerless, for they had various crystals that were energized by the powerful charges of lightning that they attracted. These particular crystals were, in turn, used to energize the six bodily Gates and keep them open. These same crystals were also capable of being programmed for various other purposes.

Lightning Chant
(for personal inner energy and power)

Light of Power. Lance of Light.
Touch this crystal stone.
Send its life in arrows through,
My sacred grounds within.

Send the Light. Send the Power.
Touch this crystal stone.
Touch this body. Touch this spirit.
Keep the sacred Life alive.

On the first eve of each month, a community dance was performed for the sole purpose of honoring the Creator. This was a very solemn occasion that was filled with high respect and sacredness. It was a slow dance done in a circle representing the Hoop of all Life and the repeating cycles of their spirits' inherent destiny toward God. Everyone in the community participated; old ones, mothers with babes in arms, children and men. It was a simple dance, yet the purpose was profound.

Spirit-Of-All Dance of Honor
(for The One)

Life Giver. Life Maker.
Healer. Creator. The One.
We honor you with our hearts and souls.
We live for the harmony of all.

Life Giver. Life Maker.
Healer. Creator. The One.
We follow all the Sacred Ways,
Each night and all our days.

Life Giver. Life Maker.
Healer. Creator. The One.
We thank you for the Gift of Life.
And pray for our return.

The Sky — *universe* to the Anasazi — was perceived as the domain of their star ancestors; therefore, the sky symbolized the Source of their intelligence and star knowledge. When chanting the Grandfather Sky Chant, the people were, in reality, not referencing an entity per se, but rather their pathway to home.

Grandfather Sky Chant

Grandfather, Grandfather Sky.
I thank you for your gifts.
I thank you for your Power Ways.
And honor your old, old spirit.

Grandfather, Grandfather Sky.
I honor your many faces shown.
I honor your Sacred Ways.
And I honor your wise Spirit.

The Spirit Clan viewed the earth as an aged, wise woman who nurtured and provided for all the life living upon her breast. They cared very much for the earth and, therefore, chanted a prayer for her continued health and protection.

Grandmother Earth Chant

Grandmother Earth.
Grandmother of All.
I honor your old, old spirit.
I honor your Sacred Ways.

Grandmother Earth.
Grandmother of All.
Thank you for your many gifts.
And my heart is full with love.

Grandmother Earth.
Grandmother of All.
I pray for your protection.
And I pray for your Living Way.

The Cloud Way Chant was recited for the purpose of bringing clouds to relieve extended periods of heat. This chant was intoned while holding up two specific crystals. Any adult in the clan was capable of performing this and the rite was not solely given to the Clan Elder or medicine person to do. This rite had to be coordinated though because if too many individuals decided to perform it simultaneously, a deluge resulted.

Cloud Way Chant
(for heat relief)

Grandfather Sky.
Sky Maker.
Blow your clouds this way.
Bring the shade. Bring the clouds,
Over us this day.

Grandfather Sky.
Sky Maker.
Blow away the heat.
Bring the shade. Blow the clouds,
Over us this day.

Spiritual enlightenment and awareness was the High Ideal of the clan community. Everything was done through attitudes and perspectives The Knowing naturally imparted. Therefore, it was a priority of the highest level for all members to maintain their level of wisdom and enlightenment, and this was accomplished by keeping the affirmation in the forefront of their minds through the daily recitation of The Knowing Way Chant.

Knowing Way Chant
(to know future with clarity)

My eyes are closed,
Yet they are opened.
I see the dark,
Yet see the Light.

I look afar,
And see the near.
I look past
And through.

I see to know,
And know to see.
Keep my closed eyes
Open so they see.

Ordinary water, whether it be from the river or rain, can have its properties altered by way of crystals. These altered waters can then be vibrationally aligned to an illness, thus creating a healing. The Water Way Chant accompanied the process.

Water Way Chant

(to create healing waters)

Sacred Stone. Stone of Crystal.
Touch these waters with your Power.
Gift them with your strength and light.
Make them flow with Healing Life.

Sacred Stone. Stone of Crystal.
Touch these waters with your Power.
Stone of Life. Living Stone.
Touch these waters with your Power.

When a communicated message was received that indicated a star relation visitation, the community became very excited and, as a group, gathered in the Commons and whispered the Brother Coming Prayer for their relatives' safe journey to earth. Since these visitations weren't frequent, every heart pounded with the joy and excitement of again seeing friends and loved ones from afar.

Brothers Coming Prayer
(for Star Brothers' safe journey to earth)

We pray to The One to watch over our
Star Relations and all their far journeys
Through the stars.

We pray to The One to protect our Star
Relations and keep them safe and guide
Their way.

Because the Spirit Clan was confined and bound to the earth, their only method of making personal star journeys was by way of spirit. This chant was recited as a precursor to an individual's spirit travel to the stars.

Star Journey Chant
(for spirit journeys to distant stars)

Spirit with Wings.
Spirit with Power.
Rise and spread your wings.
Rise like smoke.
Rise like mist,
To the Trail of Stars.
Spirit with Wings.
Spirit with Power.
Rise and spread your wings.
Rise up quiet.
Rise up strong.
Rise to walk the stars.

Crystals were a precious and most sacred aspect of lives because they were the only remnants of their former home. Each household or individual dwelling had crystals that were programmed with information equivalent to a modern encyclopedia, and it was all members' responsibility to continue their own learning and expand their minds' potential. The time for personal education followed the noonday meal when all retired to their dwellings for an hour before their crystals.

The Talking Stone Chant preceded this education period of higher learning.

Talking Stone Chant
(for clarity of crystal communications)

Talking Stone. Wisdom Crystal.
Speak to open ears.
Show these eyes,
Show this one,
Wisdom of The One.

Talking Stone. Wisdom Crystal.
Help me know the Way.
Help me learn.
Help me grow,
With Wisdom of The One.

The Calling Nature Chant was spoken aloud whenever the need arose to invoke the weather's aid. This could be for the halting or calling of snow in winter or rain in other seasons. It could be used for the purpose of calling warm winds or specialized air currents. Any natural aspect of the earth's weather could be called up by the combined use of the correct crystal and the Calling Nature Chant.

Calling Nature Chant
(Weather Prayer)

Spirits of Nature.
Nature Spirits.
Hear my voice.
Hear my call.
Come to help us.
Come to help us.

Spirits of Nature.
Nature Spirits.
Hear my voice.
Hear my call.
We need your Power.
We call your Power.

It was known that one's spirit leaves the physical body upon the occasion of death. It was also known that not all spirits journey directly to their destination and, therefore, become trapped in the lower dimensional fields of vibrations and become lost. The Ghost Prayer was solely for lost spirits to be directed home.

Ghost Prayer
(for lost spirits)

I pray for all the ghosts who wander the Trails
Of Shadowland.

I pray for all the lost spirits who wander in
Confusion and pain.
May you find your way into the Light,
And sleep on bed of Home.

May you awake before The One,
And live in lasting Peace.

The Anasazi were fully aware of all other people who were natives of earth at the time of their own existence. They knew of all the tribes extending from North America through to South America and prayed for their welfare and particularly for their societal development.

All Tribes Prayer
(for all Native People)

I pray for all the native nations who dwell
Upon this land.

I pray they dwell within the Hoop and Circle
Of Unity and Harmony.

May their Ways be straight
And their Paths be true.
May their days and nights be blessed.

May their children grow in light and love,
And may their Power hold strong.

The Last Journey Chant had no associated ceremony attached to it, but every clan member held thoughts of home in their heart. So then, this was a silent, personal mantra-type chant that each held dear. They frequently repeated this over and over, again and again in their minds as they went about their daily chores. It was especially comforting to recite as one fell asleep at night.

Last Journey Chant

Our hearts wait.
Our hearts pray.
And spirits hold the words,
Of journeys back to Home.

Our eyes look up.
Our eyes search.
And spirits watch the sky,
For the Trail back to Home.

Our ears listen.
Our ears strain.
And spirits hear the sounds,
Of thunder that takes us Home.

Whenever a clan member was experiencing grief, sorrow or a sadness of the heart, there were words that, when chanted, helped to ease the personal pain. This is a chant performed by oneself for oneself. It was known that personal grief and sorrow needed to be expressed and released lest it become internalized and become a dangerous thing.

Broken Heart Chant
(for ease of personal grief)

Spirits of the Heart.
Hear my cries.
Hear my sorrow.
Come to take the pain from me,
And heal my broken heart.

Spirits of the Heart.
See my falling tears.
Feel my deep grief.
Come to take the hurt from me,
And heal my broken heart.

The Sacred Mesa Song was an individual song, yet could be heard whispered from the mouths of every clan member; even small children knew of the Sacred Seventh Mesa. The song was for protection and invincibility.

The Sacred Seventh Mesa is where treasures of wisdom were hidden after the Star People gathered them together. The Anasazi Spirit Clan, in cooperation with their Starborn relations, worked to hone out fine chambers and hall corridors beneath the Seventh Mesa where ancient records were kept.

Sacred Mesa Song
(for protection of the Seventh Mesa)

Standing Stones.
Singing Stones.
Spirits of the Night.
Watch with Spirit Eyes.
Listen with Spirit Ears.
And guard the Sacred Mesa.

Standing Stones.
Singing Stones.
Spirits of the Night.
Watch. Listen. Guard.
The Sacred Seventh Mesa.

During the colder days of winter months, a dance was performed for the purpose of bringing warming winds to chase away the cold. This was accompanied by a simple ceremony the Chief Clan Elder did with a weather-programmed crystal.

Warm Wind Dance Chant
(a cold winter song)

Wind Spirit.
Spirit of Breath.
Blow summer winds.
Blow desert winds.
Blow warm winds our way.

Wind Spirit.
Spirit of Breath.
Blow away the chill.
Blow away the cold.
Blow the winter away.

The Man Time Chant was voiced by a boy during his Man Time Ceremony which was a walk out of boyhood into manhood. This was the crossing over into the adult world where new responsibilities and more serious concerns were expected to be shouldered. It was a proud time for the "new" man. It was a proud time for everyone as they welcomed him into the circle of adults.

Man Time Chant
(a boy's coming into manhood)

Grandfather. Oh, Grandfather.
See I am a man.
The boy had fled.
The boy is gone.
A man had come this day.

Grandfather. Oh, Grandfather.
Hear my new man voice.
I speak with Power.
I speak with Truth.
A man has come this day.

The Woman Time Chant was recited by a girl when she had her Woman Time Ceremony and walked out of girlhood into womanhood. The precise time for each girl's readiness was solely left up to the Women's Medicine Woman who had been tutoring the clan's girls. When a girl was perceived to have reached a certain level of understanding and maturity, the Women's Medicine Woman called for a Woman Time Ceremony for her. The entire clan participated and it was a joyous occasion for celebration.

Woman Time Chant
(a girl's coming into womanhood)

Grandmother. Oh, Grandmother.
I am a woman this day.
The girl has fled.
The girl is gone.
A woman has come this day.

Grandmother. Oh, Grandmother.
Hear my new woman voice.
I speak of Love.
I speak of Wisdom.
A woman has come this day.

The Sacred Shield Prayer was said by all clan members for the purpose of strengthening the spiritual force field that acted as a sacred shield over the entire community. This shield was not only for physical protection, but because they knew the number of their allotted years, it was primarily for historical protection.

Sacred Shield Prayer
(historical protection of Anasazi)

May the Sacred Clan Shield live in the Power
Of its Light,
And may the Force be filled with lasting Strength
To blanket the People's life.
May the People's Way be protected through Time,
And may Time hold its Power strong.

From the time clan members were small children, they were taught the importance of knowing oneself — truly knowing self. It was believed that nothing outside yourself could be really known unless you first knew yourself. This meant knowing and understanding how one thinks, perceives, uses reasoning and logic. It meant understanding one's attitudes and moods, and the reasons that instigated them. Knowing self was an elementary tenet that all began to strive for even as they took their first steps, said their first words; for mothers and teachers were always asking the children why they thought this or that, and children learned early that there were reasons to all the whys.

Heart Knowing chant
(to know self)

Help me to see.
The face of me.
Help me to hear
The voice of me.

Help me to know
The heart of me.
Help me to be
The spirit of me.

Cedar smoke was believed to be a spiritually cleansing agent. In the Anasazi dwellings, each household had a small altar used for various purposes; one being the burning of cedar to shield the home from dark forces. This was done each morning and evening.

Cedar Burning Prayer
(for protection against dark spirits)

Cedar Spirit.
Spirit of Light.
Burn, burn bright.

Cedar Spirit.
Spirit of Light.
Chase away
Dark Ones of Night.

Cedar Spirit.
Spirit of Light.
Burn, burn bright.

Although it was foreseen that some clan members would choose to remain behind and integrate into other native tribes when the main clan body left the community, it was important to keep everyone together until the parting time arrived. And so there was a prayer for this purpose that was recited by all members of the clan as they gathered in a circle once each month.

Together Time Chant
(for keeping clan together)

Spirit Clan.
Spirit Tribe.
People of the Spirit.
We are Ones
Of The One,
Circle of the Circle.

Spirit Clan.
Spirit Tribe.
People of the Spirit.
We are Ones
Of The One,
Nation of the Spirit.

Keep us whole.
Keep the Circle.
Keep us of the Nation.
Keep the Ones of The One.

Like the society members who had specialized chants, prayers and songs to help them remain center-focused on their specific tasks or talents, so too did the Bread Makers pray for loving energy to flow through their hands. They sang of their work bringing health, sustenance and happiness to all they nourished with their bread.

Bread Making Song

Grandmother. Oh, Grandmother.
Giver of this seed.
Guide my hands to make this bread,
A gift from my own heart.

Grandmother. Oh, Grandmother.
Giver of this flour.
Guide my heart to make this bread,
A gift from my own hands.

The Anasazi were excellent listeners, not only to each other's words but also to nature. They knew that nature speaks and they were perceptive listeners. When individuals were losing the ear for nature, they knew they were slipping out of sync with it and that was a very undesirable state to be in. When this happened, one silently prayed for realignment and quickly visited the Clan Shaman for a spiritual adjustment of their auric field.

Open Ear Prayer
(to be a perceptive listener of nature)

May my ears be open to hear the sounds
Of voices near and far.

May I listen well to hear the sounds
Of nature's spoken word.

And may I never close my ears
To the voice of other's hearts.

The Remembering Way Chant was recited whenever a clan individual felt spiritually prompted to recall past lives for the purpose of overcoming current blocks, illnesses or problems. The Clan Shaman assisted with this highly personal process as he himself accompanied the individual into the past while still maintaining a firm and strong foothold in the present.

Remembering Way Chant
(to remember one's spiritual wholeness)

Spirit Wings. Spirit Wings.
Take me back to see,
Take me back to know,
The part of me I need to be.

Spirit Wings. Spirit Wings.
Rise into the Trail to Time.
Rise into the Time Ago,
And let me see a face of mine.

Spirit Wings. Spirit Wings.
Gather all your Power.
Rise Above and Fly Within,
Journey far into your Power.

All clan members of the community had their own medicine bundles that contained unique objects that were personally sacred to them. Even children were encouraged to make their own bundles and secret away their personalized objects. In this way, the sacredness of nature and its powers were ingrained and nurtured from a very young age.

The Medicine Power Prayer was whispered over one's own medicine bundle before it was opened — each time.

Medicine Power Prayer
(said over one's personal medicine bundle)

Power Spirit.
Spirits of Power
Protect this Sacred Bundle and all objects within it.
Keep the Power strong.
Keep my medicine alive.

May my medicine always be strong.
May my Medicine Power never fail.

The Spirit Clan dwellings were decorated with hanging sage in doorways, windows and in every corner. Sage also was to the right and left of the home altar. Sage was believed to protect the dwelling and all living within it from inner negativity. This does not refer to dark spirits, but rather dark forces that can get hold of one within.

Sage Hanging Prayer
(for home protection)

Grandmother. Oh, Grandmother Earth.
I hang your sage and have faith in its spirit's power.

With this sage I make this dwelling safe.
With this sage I repel all dark forces.

Grandmother. Oh, Grandmother.
May the spirit of this sage dwell within this house.

The planet was in a state of motion. Grandmother Earth breathed. When she held her breath, great pressure built up beneath the surface and she would release her air in a powerful whoosh that exploded up out of the land in the form of volcanos and earthquakes. The Anasazi knew and understood the Earth Mother's need to breathe in a regular pattern so her energies would not build up; therefore they had a dance and chant for this energy release from within the earth that, at night, could be seen as a faint blue light that came as flashes from the earth.

Light Calling Dance Chant
(for earth's energy pressure release)

Earth Spirit. Grandmother.
Breathe deep.
Release your breath.
Breathe deep.

Grandmother. Earth Spirit.
Release your energy.
Open your soul.
Sound your heartbeats.

Earth Spirit. Grandmother.
Breathe deep.
Release your breath.
Breathe deep. Breathe deep.

Prayers for the newly deceased were sacred words directed to the freed spirit. These words were meant to help the spirit recall its physical death and to remind it of its journey direction and purpose so it wouldn't be confused and lose its way. Because the Spirit Clan came from a highly developed civilization, the people were well versed in the truths of spirit realities.

Spirit Journey Prayer
(for the newly dead)

Old Spirit of our clan.
Old Spirit of the People.
Spread your Spirit Wings and rise free.
Spread your Spirit Wings and fly high.
Old Spirit of our clan.
Old Spirit of the People.
Open your Spirit Eyes and look ahead.
Open your Spirit Eyes and don't look back.

Old Spirit of our clan.
Old Spirit of the People.
Walk straight upon the Star Trail.
Walk straight into the Lights.

The Give-Away Dance Song was performed every six months when the Give-Away Ceremony was celebrated. This was a festive and joyous occasion when all clan members cooked something special to share at the banquet dinner. During the day, people gave away handicrafts they'd made. The highlight was when they chose their most prized possession and then gave it to another. This was to show their love for one another in conjunction with exemplifying their priorities that placed spiritual attitudes above the material aspects of life.

Give-Away Dance Song
(a potlatch and sharing song)

This day, each day,
Rain and sun,
Snow Moon, Warm Moon,
Nighttime and noon,
We share ourselves,
We give ourselves,
We are all ones of One.

Give-Away, Give-Away.
The joy of Giving Away.

I give to you.
You give to me.
We give to them.
They give to us.
We share ourselves.
We give ourselves.
We are all ones of One.

The Star Power Chant could be uttered by any member of the clan community. Even small children recognized the importance of their star relation's imperative need to remain undetected in this new and strange land. They were different from the earth's native people and, although the star visitors utilized vehicles across the Anasazi lands, their prayers were clearly effective due to present-day consternation over the "road tracks" discerned by puzzled archaeologists.

Star Power Chant

(to keep Star Brothers undetected)

Grandfather, speak to The One.
Take to him our prayer.
We pray for our Brothers' safety,
And protection in the air.

Grandfather, speak to The One.
Take to him our prayer.
We pray for our Brothers' journeys,
And pray they remain unseen.

The Anasazi were cognizant of all lifeforms that existed upon and beneath the earth they now called home for a time. These lifeforms were all inclusive, thereby encompassing "intelligent" beings as well. Intelligent beings, as the clan knew, meant those of every form seen and unseen. Yet all the Unseen were indeed seen frequently by the Spirit Clan for they often communicated with those of modern-day myth. Ones such as these were those currently termed Sasquatch.

Big Brother Prayer
(for Sasquatch and others)

Spirits of the Big Ones.
Spirits of the Wood.
May Grandmother keep you in her arms,
And safe from all harm.

Spirits of the Wood.
Spirits of the Big Ones.
We pray for your protection.
We pray for your sacred Way.

When a clan couple decided they wanted to spend the rest of their lives together, there was a span of two months before they were actually married. The beginning of this time period would be compared to an engagement period today. The couple announced their intentions and a Blanket Dance Ceremony was performed. The entire community gathered on the Common Grounds for the festive celebration. Food was plentiful and the day was spent playing games and visiting. After the banquet, when the sun went down, the couple wrapped a single blanket about their shoulders and danced around the central fire while the community sang the Blanket Dance Song to them.

Blanket Dance Song
(for an engaged couple)

See these two,
Who dance as one.
See these two,
Who walk as one.

Hear these two,
Who laugh as one.
Hear these two,
Who speak as one.

Under one blanket,
Under one blanket,
Walking together,
Dancing together.

Sharing words.
Sharing trails.
Making certain,
Hearts are true.

Moccasins were not the usual form of footwear for the Anasazi, for they preferred their own traditional style of soft sandals or a cloth-type of durable material that was brought by their star relations. Frequently going barefoot was an expression of freedom they enjoyed.

Whether their footwear was styled from leather or fabric, the Makers recited an associated prayer during the creation process so that all footfalls would be placed true upon each wearer's destined trail.

Moccasin Making Prayer
(for walking straight paths)

Grandmother. Oh, Grandmother.
Guide my hands this day.
I give my work,
And voice my words,
In a sacred way.

Grandmother. Oh, Grandmother.
I pray my work will guide one's feet
Upon their destined Trail.
And may they walk with gentle steps,
Through their sacred Paths.

Being temporary earth residents with a prescribed visitation time allotted to them, the Anasazi People perceived the planet through reverent and loving eyes. Therefore it was naturally inherent for them to pray for the continuance of earth's existence. They knew the earth would continue, but their prayers were directed for a peaceful and harmonious existence.

Many Suns Prayer
(for the Earth Mother's future)

Earth Spirit.
Spirit of our Grandmother.
May you live in peace and harmony,
And dwell in everyone's heart.

Earth Spirit.
Spirit of our Grandmother.
May you live in youthful beauty,
And receive respect and honor.

Earth Spirit.
Spirit of our Grandmother.
May your sweet face remain unchanged through
time,
And may all life give thanks for your being.

Protecting the community young ones was a high priority, and along with that came many various associated responsibilities. But most enjoyable was sitting beside a sleeping child and singing the lullaby called Child Sleep Song.

Child Sleep Song
(a lullaby)

Sleep Little One.
Sleep in peace.
You are loved, Little One.
You are loved.

Sleep Little One.
Sleep in peace.
You are never alone.
You are never alone.

Sleep, Little One.
Sleep in peace.
Dream of Sunshine.
Dream of Starshine.

It wasn't enough that prayers, chants and songs were intoned for nearly every conceivable occasion and purpose, for the Spirit Clan thought it also important to insure their voices were heard. Therefore, a whispered prayer was infused with their altar smoke beseeching The One to hear all their prayers. This specific request was called the Rising Smoke Prayer.

Rising Smoke Prayer
(for all Anasazi prayers to be heard)

Grandfather. Message Taker.
Give our prayers to The One.
We pray all our prayers reach his ears.
We pray no words go unheard.

Grandfather. Message Taker.
Give our prayers to The One.
Your People walk the Sacred Way,
And follow the Guiding Star.

Grandfather. Message Taker.
Give our prayers to The One.
We send our words on rising smoke,
So no clan prayers go unheard.

The Anasazi People didn't need to recite a prayer to insure the continuance of their loving nature, but because they were such a compassionate and spiritually conscientious society, they desired to always maintain their ingrained attitudes in the new land. They needlessly feared the possibility of straying away from their star traditions because of the great distance that separated them from home. So then, they voiced the Loving Way Prayer to personally insure their own hearts and minds.

Loving Way Prayer
(to keep the People loving in all ways)

Keep us kind
With open hearts.
Keep us kind
With open eyes.

Keep us loving
With open hearts.
Keep us loving
With open eyes.

Kind. Loving.
Let our Way be
All days full
Of the Loving Way.

The winter months could be hard on the clan if they hadn't provided plentiful supplies during the warm seasons. However, this was never a true concern for them because they planned well. Still they prayed for their own continued foresight. The Snow Moon Song was as much for all life forms as it was for themselves, but it especially addressed all the nature beings who lived naturally upon and within the earth who depended on the earth's gifts of bounty for their sustenance and warmth.

Snow Moon Song
(for plentiful provisions for the People and nature beings)

Grandmother. Spirit of Earth.
Winter snow and bitter cold has come.
Watch the Little Ones of wood and plain.
Keep them in your care.
Grandmother. Spirit of Earth.
Cold Moon sheds a chilling light.
Provide for us and give to them,
All your warmth and love.

Being deeply compassionate and highly sensitive, the members of the Spirit Clan possessed great empathy for one another. Because of this, another's inner sorrow or state of grief rarely passed unnoticed by others in the community. So then, whenever someone's sorrow was felt, the Bad Heart Prayer was said for them. This was to help their sorrow by sharing the pain of it.

Bad Heart Prayer
(to ease another's grief-filled heart)

Another has a Bad Heart.
I feel it in my soul.
I wish to ease the sorrow,
That another holds within.

My spirit takes away the pain,
My spirit cries the tears,
Of another with a Bad Heart,
That I feel inside my soul.

I share the pain,
The tears, the fears,
Of another with a Bad Heart,
That I feel inside my soul.

The coming of twilight was a quiet and tranquil time when various special prayers were said. One of these was the Twilight Chant that prayed for peace to reign throughout the coming night. This peace was not confined to the community, but included all other beings, both of the human and nature kind. Animals too were drawn into this Hoop of Peace that the Twilight Chant included.

Twilight Chant

Silent Time.
Sacred Time.
Time for going Within.
Time for seeing in the Dusk,
The Spirit of our Trust.

Silent Time.
Sacred Time.
Time for thoughts of Peace.
Time for prayers for Thankfulness,
For all of Life's night Restfulness.

In the darkness of each new moon, the clan community gathered in the Common Grounds to perform a special dance. Much drumming accompanied the chanting. Then, as one, all clan members sat in a circle to gaze at the winking stars above and silently contemplate what their starborn heritage personally meant to them.

New Moon Dance Chant
(a celebration of clan's Star Heritage)

Stars Above.
Spirit's Light.
I think of you this night.
Starborn Ways.
Heritage Ways.
I think of you this night.

Stars Above.
Spirit's Light.
You live within my heart.
You dwell within my soul.
And I live in the warming love,
That shines from the One Above.

Beneath the bright silver light of each full moon, the clan community gathered in the Common Ground area to hear the Chief Clan Elder recite the prophecy of their starborn ancestors. They called this prophecy the Anasazi Prophecy, for it dealt with the present community and their foreseen future. When the recitation was concluded, all whispered the Full Moon prayer as an amen to the Elder's words.

Full Moon Prayer
(for fulfillment of the Anasazi prophesy)

We are The People.
The Starborn Tribe.
Born of the Stars.

We are the Protectors of the Wisdom.
The Watchers of the Seventh Mesa.
The Spirit Clan.

We are The People.
Born of the Stars.
The Starborn Tribe.

About The Artist

A native of New Mexico, Ann Marie's visionary/fantasy paintings are known throughout the country. "Anasazi" came to her while she and Mary Summer Rain were visiting together at an art show in Colorado. Ann Marie was delighted when asked if it could be used as a cover for this book. Prints are available from: Touch of Fantasy Art Studio, P. O. Box 1025, Elephant Butte, New Mexico 87935.

Hampton Roads publishes a variety of books on metaphysical, spiritual, health-related, and general interest subjects. Would you like to be notified as we publish new books in your area of interest? If you would like a copy of our latest catalog, just call toll-free, (800) 766-8009, or send your name and address to:

Hampton Roads Publishing Company, Inc.
891 Norfolk Square
Norfolk, VA 23502